ALTER- NATIVES
TO
THE
Peace Corps

A Directory of Third World and US Volunteer Opportunities

Food First
Institute for Food and Development Policy

FOOD FIRST

The Institute for Food and Development Policy (FOOD FIRST) is a nonprofit research and education center, which, since its founding in 1975, has been dedicated to identifying the root causes of hunger in the United States and around the world. Financed by thousands of members, with modest support from foundations and churches, FOOD FIRST speaks with a strong, independent voice, free of ideological formulas and vested interests.

In over 50 countries and in 20 languages, FOOD FIRST provides a wide array of educational tools—books, articles, slide shows, films, and curricula for elementary schools and high schools—to lay the groundwork for a more democratically controlled food system that will meet the needs of all.

To order additional copies of this book or to receive a free
catalog of resources call or write:
Food First Books
145 Ninth Street
San Francisco, CA 94103
(415) 864-8555

Please add 15 percent for postage and handling ($1.00 minimum)
Bulk discounts available

TO ORDER CALL TOLL FREE 800-888-3314

Table of Contents

Acknowledgments

Alternatives to the Peace Corps has been published in response to the numerous inquiries Food First receives from individuals seeking opportunities to gain third world experience but not interested in working with a government-sponsored agency such as the Peace Corps.

Becky Buell, a staff member at Food First from 1985 to 1988, researched and wrote the original edition in 1986 with the assistance of Kari Hamerschlag, a Food First intern. The tremendous demand for the booklet created a continuing need to have it revised and updated periodically, and Becky subsequently supervised the expanded second and third editions.

This fourth edition was revised and edited by Katherine Castro, a Food First intern working under the supervision of staff member Harriet Y. Wright

We would like to thank the many other volunteers and interns who have assisted us in this project over the years, and to acknowledge the cooperation of the many organizations that are listed in the resource guide.

Introduction

Since 1961, more than 122,000 Americans have worked abroad through the Peace Corps voluntary service program. Thousands more have been volunteers with church, government, and private organizations.

Many people choose to work abroad to address hunger and poverty in the third world. The media images of famine are only the most vivid reminders of the wide discrepancies between our own standard of living and that of the world's majority. Outraged by the injustice of world hunger, some people are motivated to take direct and immediate action.

But how can we be assured that our actions are truly helping the poor? What is an appropriate role for outsiders working to end hunger and poverty abroad?

Every voluntary service organization has its own answers to these questions. While most use similar phrases—"helping the poor help themselves," "building local self-reliance," or "inspiring participatory development"—each organization has its own understanding of the causes of poverty and the volunteer's role in addressing those problems.

At the Institute for Food and Development Policy (Food First), we have found that world hunger is complicated by misunderstanding and false assumptions about effective solutions. Our analyses of food and population patterns throughout the world have led us to conclude that hunger is not a problem of scarcity, overpopulation, or natural disasters. Neither is hunger caused by poor people's lack of know-how. Rather, hunger is rooted in a system of food production, distribution, and consumption that concentrates control and benefits in the hands of a few. (See Food First's book, *World Hunger: Twelve Myths*, by Frances Moore Lappé and Joseph Collins.)

Once we recognize that hunger is not created by deficiencies on the part of the poor, our role as outsiders changes. Rather than seeing ourselves as the problem-solvers bringing our models of development to the third world, we see ourselves as participants in a process

1

of change that is defined by the poor. We can contribute to this process in many ways, if we understand that solutions must originate from the people who will be most affected.

Alternatives to the Peace Corps brings together resources and information that will help the prospective volunteer find an appropriate placement. Our intention is not to indict the Peace Corps or judge the personal commitments of Peace Corps volunteers, but to respond to frequent requests for guidance on how to work in the third world. Many of these requests have come from people—some of them returned Peace Corps volunteers—who believe that U.S. foreign policy has a destructive impact in the third world. They have decided, therefore, that they cannot ethically work for an arm of the U.S. government abroad, even if their particular service would in no way be political. *Alternatives to the Peace Corps* is the first guide of its kind to directly address these questions and pose alternative options for voluntary service.

Why Work Abroad?

Before making a commitment to work abroad, it is important to clarify your motives. While you may be drawn to voluntary service by a desire to help the poor, you may be ill-equipped to do so. Most volunteers will find that the people they have been sent to help are far more sophisticated than any foreign "expert." Even highly qualified professionals can undermine local development efforts. As an outsider, the volunteer may misinterpret local needs, disregard local organizations, and become more harmful than helpful.

Learning the dynamics of a community is the greatest challenge to a foreign volunteer. As such, the volunteer's most appropriate role is that of a student. Working abroad can be a vehicle to enhance your understanding of the world, the forces that keep people impoverished, and to appreciate the richness of other cultures. These lessons can have a long-lasting impact on your life. For many, working abroad marks the beginning of a lifelong commitment to ending poverty and hunger.

If your concern is to improve your qualifications for a career in development, an unconventional work experience may enhance your candidacy. Voluntary service overseas is often seen as the primary way to gain experience for such a career. But there are many other options available: alternative study tours, short-term work projects, international educational programs, and community service projects in low-income communities in the United States.

At Food First, we remind concerned U.S. citizens who want to help the poor in the third world that the best place to start is here at home. By working to make U.S. policies more accountable to poor people, by stopping military intervention throughout the world, and by working to end U.S. economic and military support of repressive regimes, we can help create the political climate in which grassroots efforts can flourish both here and abroad. Work in the third world can deepen our understanding of this responsibility and therefore make our work at home more effective.

Common Questions

What are the options for working abroad?

If your objective in going abroad is to gain greater understanding of third world problems, volunteering with an international development or relief organization is not the only option. While voluntary service organizations often provide the easiest route to working overseas, their programs may place volunteers in uneasy political or social situations. Many programs expect the volunteer to direct the projects of a village or to influence the decisions of a group based on Western values. These difficulties may be avoided if you research the voluntary service organization extensively prior to making a commitment.

Some of the most exciting possibilities for working abroad can be designed independently according to your interests and beliefs. One option is to identify a group or organization in a country of interest and communicate with it directly about working as a volunteer. By researching grassroots organizations in the third world beforehand, you will learn about many of the complicated issues surrounding development efforts and know better where you would like to focus your energies. You will also be in a better position to assess the skills you have to offer.

Identifying local grassroots organizations calls for thorough investigative research. You can begin by reviewing alternative publications, development journals, and the annual reports of organizations that fund projects, such as Oxfam, Grassroots International, War on Want (U.K.), and World Neighbors. We have listed several publications in the resource guide that catalog grassroots organizations throughout the world. But this is only the first step. Most important, you will need to contact the organizations to determine whether they would be interested in hosting a volunteer.

Another option is to go overseas as a student. A number of universities offer study abroad programs that provide an opportunity to learn about the political, economic, and social climate of a given country. As many of these programs are academically oriented and often overlook the concerns of poor people, you will need to seek out local individuals and groups directly involved with the poor.

If you are still interested in working with a grassroots organization, these contacts will be key in your search for an appropriate placement.

A long-term commitment may not be necessary. If your goal is to gain a better understanding of the world and to learn from the experiences of others, then another option is to choose one or several short-term trips or work exchange programs.

There are a number of groups that conduct "reality tours" in the third world. These are socially responsible educational tours to provide participants firsthand experience of the political, economic, and social structures that create or sustain hunger, poverty, and environmental degradation. These tours offer an opportunity to meet people with diverse perspectives on agriculture, development, and the environment. They often include the opportunity to stay with local people, visit rural areas and meet with grassroots organizers. Such tours can alter your understanding of hunger and poverty in the third world and direct you to areas where you can best work for democratic social change. The resource guide includes a list of groups that conduct such tours.

In any case, whether you choose a volunteer program, a tour, or go on your own, it is essential to do your homework beforehand. Read as much as possible about the country—including its political climate, learn about groups working in the area, write in advance to groups that interest you, and talk to people at home who know about the area you are considering.

How can I finance my stay if I don't go through an established program?

For many people who want to work abroad, financing is the greatest obstacle. It is often the primary reason for going through a voluntary service organization. However, there are alternative funding sources to consider for overseas work. Just as we invest in a college education, a home, or car, we can invest in our education through travel abroad.

Students may have opportunities for financial assistance through scholarships, fellowships, or loans. You may find funds to pay travel expenses by going through a university or language-study program. Some university departments have research funds that are available to both undergraduate and graduate students. A public library, a career service center, or a specialized library like the Foundation

Center, based in Washington, D.C., with branches throughout the country, are sources for information on grants and loans.

There are many untapped resources in local governments, private associations, and church groups. The Rotary Club, for example, offers scholarships for foreign travel. Many churches will support their parishioners if they agree to do educational work upon their return.

Friends and relatives are another possible source of funds. You may be able to arrange a personal loan or an exchange. A woman who traveled throughout Central America for a year started her own newsletter and asked friends and family to subscribe to help subsidize her living expenses.

The first source is your own bank account. Look at the possibility of working to save money for a trip. The primary expense will be your plane fare; living in the third world, especially in rural areas, can be extremely affordable. If you can arrange an internship or a work exchange (e.g., teaching English) for room and board, your living expenses can be kept to a minimum.

What kind of support will I have if I go on my own?

The idea of going to an unknown place, with no program for guidance or support, can be scary. But if you have prepared yourself ahead of time by learning about the country, the language, and the problems of the poor, an institutional support group will seem less important. The people you are working with will become your support system, not a U.S.-based organization that has little connection to your immediate situation.

Do I need technical skills to work abroad?

Generally, the demand for unskilled volunteers is low. Several years ago the tendency was to import development professionals to solve local problems. But now more local people are employed for both skilled and unskilled work. In considering volunteer opportunities, it is important to ask if you would be taking a job that could be done by a local person.

In any work experience local people can best define your role in their organization. Let them know what your skills are and let them decide how they can best put those skills to use. Someone who went to work with a community organization in Mexico learned that his most useful skill was puppet-making. He didn't know before he arrived in Mexico that street theater is a popular form of political communication. When a local clinic learned that he was an artist and an actor they suggested he help them communicate health care information through puppet shows.There are many organizations that take volunteers for specific technical skills, such as construction, health care and agriculture. The resource section lists a number of these organizations.

Lessons From the Peace Corps

Deciding to work abroad is a difficult decision in itself. Yet even more difficult are the myriad choices in arranging where to go, with what organization, with what funds, and for what purpose.

The most common solution to this dilemma is to choose an overseas volunteer program such as the Peace Corps in which all arrangements are made by the sponsoring organization. Many organizations provide training, health and accident insurance, travel expenses, and even a stipend.

The solution seems simple enough. But these programs are not always as straightforward as they seem. The countries in which an organization works, the projects it supports, and the role of its volunteers have many political, social, and cultural implications. Volunteers are not merely well-meaning individuals; they are representatives of the organizations that sponsor them. As such, volunteers are expected to communicate the governmental, religious or private values and objectives of the organization they represent.

For example, the Peace Corps, the most renowned of the voluntary service organizations, is an agency of the United States government. The Peace Corps volunteer is part of the "country team" of the U.S. State Department, accountable to the U.S. ambassador in the foreign country. As such, the Peace Corps is inevitably linked to U.S. foreign policy objectives. The Peace Corps was established in 1961 with the expressed purpose of countering Soviet cultural and political influence in the developing world. Upon its conception, Senator Hubert Humphrey explained that "this program is to be an arm of the total foreign policy of the United States to combat the virus of Communist totalitarianism." The role of volunteers in this effort is reflected in amendment 8(c) of the Peace Corps legislation, which ordered that trainees be instructed in the "philosophy, strategy, tactics, and menace of Communism." These are the underpinnings of a volunteer's placement whether or not she or he agrees that communism is a menace in the third world.

However, the Peace Corps must be credited for enabling thousands of American citizens to see firsthand the realities of poverty and injustice in the third world. This experience has even led some returned Peace Corps volunteers to work against U.S. foreign policy—the very policy that allowed them to go to the third world as volunteers!

Digging Up the Facts

No matter which voluntary service organization you are considering, get answers to questions such as these before you make a commitment:

- What is the political or religious affiliation of the organization? In the organization's bylaws, is the express or strongly implied purpose of the organization to convert or influence the poor to adopt new cultural, economic, or social values?

- Who funds the organization? Do the funding sources have political or religious affiliations that may bias the organization's programs?

- Is the organization working with local or national governments? Overtly or covertly? Under the auspices of another institution?

- In what countries does the organization have programs? In what countries does it NOT have programs, and why?

- What do former volunteers say about their experience? Did they ever feel compromised by their affiliation?

These questions are hard to answer with the information in brochures or publicity materials. Look beyond the rhetoric of the brochures. Get a list of program alumni and ask them about their experiences, write to people in the field, find out who is critical of the program and why. The reference section lists several books that take a critical look at development organizations overseas.

We compiled the list of organizations by asking these questions ourselves. We looked for groups with a reputation for supporting grassroots organizations that are addressing the political and economic causes of poverty. The resource guide provides a starting point to explore the options for working abroad. Through your own research of these organizations and others, you can choose the appropriate options available to you.

Bringing the Lessons Home

Living abroad and working with poor people to address the causes of hunger and poverty can have a long-lasting impact on your life. It can also deepen your understanding of the tremendous power the United States has over the lives of people around the world— power to make and break governments, to affect the world economy through trade, investment, and foreign aid policies, and to influence economic priorities through international aid programs such as U.S. AID, the World Bank, and the International Monetary Fund.

Going abroad will be educational, but that is only the beginning. Third world experience means taking the responsibility of bringing your experiences home. The lessons learned abroad may have direct applications: working to end hunger and poverty in our own country, pressuring the U.S. government to end its involvement with repressive regimes, stopping the militarization of the third world, and holding U.S. corporations accountable for their actions abroad.

There are many ways in which a third world experience can be translated into work at home. A Peace Corps volunteer who served with Indians in Guatemala returned to the United States and worked with Native Americans in Arizona. A health care volunteer with an international organization in Ghana found work at a free clinic in California. An agricultural extension worker who volunteered in Mozambique became active in the movement to stop U.S. support of South Africa's apartheid regime. These examples and others show that experience in a third world community is often the catalyst for taking action in our own country to create more democratic organizations and policies at the local, national, or international level, and to help ensure the survival of grassroots efforts all over the world. For many, working abroad was just the first step.

RESOURCE GUIDE

The variety of opportunities listed in this resource guide demonstrates the range of options for overseas service and education. The listings are by no means comprehensive. Many organizations are so small and take so few volunteers that they preferred not to be listed. Hundreds of other possibilities are not mentioned because they are not formal volunteer programs. Every community, school, church and labor union holds unlimited potential for developing international programs that may send delegates abroad, initiate ongoing partnership programs and offer direct assistance to third world communities. These opportunities are often the most exciting, but must be created by the volunteer.

We have compiled a select list of organizations that, in our view, place volunteers in positions that complement the work of local people and groups. Many on the list are not traditional voluntary service organizations. They may have programs that send volunteers abroad, but their main purpose is educational work in the United States. Through service and work projects, their aim is to build lasting links between communities at home and abroad. Many of the listings are programs affiliated with churches. These were selected for their commitment to the poor. People with a religious background may consider one of these organizations for short- or long-term service.

One section of the guide is dedicated to options for voluntary service in the United States. While many college graduates and job-seekers feel pressured to gain their "minimum two years overseas experience," there are numerous development opportunities here at home. Voluntary service in low-income communities in the United States can also be a valuable educational experience or qualification for future work.

Alternatives to the Peace Corps *is an ongoing project of Food First. This guide will be updated again in the future. We rely on the comments and recommendations of our readers to improve each new edition. We welcome your suggestions for changes or additions.*

Note: Most of the organizations listed in the resource guide function on very small budgets. If you are writing to request information, please enclose a self-addressed, stamped envelope.

International Voluntary Service Organizations

The following organizations offer opportunities to work with the poor in the third world. These voluntary service organizations were selected for their approach to combatting poverty, which emphasizes support of grassroots efforts to empower poor people.

American Friends Service Committee
1501 Cherry Street
Philadelphia, PA 19102-1479
(215) 241-7000

AFSC cosponsors summer community service projects of six to eight weeks with Mexican and other Latin American organizations. Approximately 50 volunteers serve with Latin Americans in small teams working and living in villages. Applicants should be 18 to 26 years old, fluent in Spanish, and have skills in construction, gardening, arts, crafts, child care, or other practical areas. A limited number of scholarships are available.

Amigos de las Americas
5618 Star Lane
Houston, TX 77057
(800) 231-7796

Young volunteers, 16 years or older, work in teams at schools, health clinics and in communities in Latin America providing health care services. In addition to supplying technical knowledge and supplies, the volunteers assume leadership roles as health educators. A network of Amigos chapters and training groups across the country conducts training prior to departure and raises funds for the majority of volunteers. Costs range from $2,200 to $3,000, depending on the area of placement. At least one year of high school Spanish is a prerequisite.

Architects and Planners in Support of Nicaragua (APSNICA)
P.O. Box 1151
Topanga, CA 90290
(213) 455-1340

APSNICA provides material and technical services to various organizations, institutes and community groups. Assistance is provided in a variety of areas such as accounting, agronomy, architecture, computer programming, construction, economics, engineering, forestry, hydrology, mechanics, nutrition, planning, social work, surveying, teaching and veterinary medicine, among others. Skill requirements and costs vary with the placement. In addition to individual placements, APSNICA facilitates work brigades and other groups interested in working in Nicaragua, and hosts delegations to Nicaragua organized by others. Volunteers pay all their own expenses.

Baseball for Peace
P.O. Box 8282
Woodland, CA 95695
(916) 661-1659

Volunteers tour Nicaragua, playing baseball with local teams and donating equipment. The aim of the project is to increase international understanding. Baseball ability and some Spanish are helpful. Volunteers stay from ten days to two weeks and pay all expenses.

Bay Area Construction Brigade to Nicaragua
P.O. Box 2963
Oakland, CA 94609
(415) 835-2511

The Brigade is currently recruiting volunteers to teach woodworking skills in a high school woodshop in the Chontales province of Nicaragua. Basic Spanish skills and the knowledge and ability to teach basic machine tool safety, operation and maintenance, and the making of simple toys and other products required. The Brigade is also recruiting volunteers to help in other construction and agricultural projects related to the school and community. Minimum teaching commitment is four months. Some financial assistance is possible.

16

Brethren Volunteer Services

451 Dundee Avenue
Elgin, IL 60120
(312) 742-5100

This Christian service program works to advocate justice, serve basic human needs, and support peacemaking. BVS places volunteers with locally sponsored church projects in Latin America, the Caribbean, the Middle East and Europe. Positions abroad last two years and begin with a three-week orientation in the United States. In addition, there are one-year programs in the United States and China. Volunteers are involved in a variety of community services, including education, health care, office/secretarial work, construction work, and ministry to children, youth, senior citizens, homeless, victims of domestic violence, prisoners, refugees, persons with AIDS and others. Some positions require knowledge of foreign language prior to orientation. Requirements for other special skills vary with assignment. Volunteers need not be Brethren or Christian but must have an interest in examining the Christian faith. A college degree or equivalent life experience is required for overseas assignments. Transportation expenses to and from the project, room and board, medical coverage and a monthly stipend of approximately $35 are provided.

Committee for Health Rights in Central America (CHRICA)

347 Dolores Street, # 210
San Francisco, CA 94110
(415) 431-7768

or

National Central American Health Rights Network

853 Broadway, #416
New York, NY 10003
(212) 420-9635

CHRICA helps medical volunteers apply for placement with the Nicaraguan Ministry of Health and directs volunteers to other opportunities in Central America. CHRICA also recruits unpaid volunteers for the following programs:

Maternal/Child Health Project. Labor and delivery nurses and midwives are needed to train women health workers in Nicaragua. Self-sufficiency and fluency in Spanish are required.

Mental Health Program for Central American Refugees. Mental health care professionals needed to work as trainers with refugees to develop a counseling program. Trainers should speak Spanish, be self-sufficient and have experience in mental health care. Spanish-speaking accredited professionals are also needed to serve as on-call counselors.

Concern/America
P.O. Box 1790
Santa Ana, CA 92702
(714) 953-8575

Concern is a hunger-relief and development organization which places volunteers in Bangladesh, El Salvador, Guatemala, Honduras, Mexico, Sierra Leone, and the Sudan. Volunteers must have a degree in public health, nutrition, agriculture, engineering, or medicine and be at least 21 years of age. Placements are for a minimum of one year. Spanish is required if working in Latin America. Room, board, round trip transportation, insurance, and a monthly stipend of $50 are provided. In addition, a repatriation allowance of $50 per month of service is placed in an account in the United States.

Cristianos por la Paz en El Salvador (CRISPAZ)
701 South Zarzamora Street
San Antonio, TX 78207
(512) 433-6185

Volunteers work for a minimum of one year with responsibilities in one or more community programs. Placements are in teaching, agriculture, health care, or pastoral ministry. Volunteers must have a sponsoring community that provides a monthly stipend and all other material needs, as well as general assistance and emotional support. Volunteers must speak Spanish and have skills relevant to the assignment.

Farmer to Farmer
Route 1, Box 7
Ridgeland, WI 54763
(715) 949-1046

Volunteers knowledgeable in dairy farming, agronomy, or veterinary medicine are sent to Nicaragua to conduct training, work on diary projects or assist in getting new projects off the ground. Length of placement is flexible. Spanish is helpful, but not required. Volunteers pay travel expenses, but room and board may be provided, depending on placement.

Father Wasson's Orphans
Nuestros Pequeños Hermanos
P.O. Box 1027
Yarnell, AZ 85362
(602) 427-3339

Volunteers work in Father Wasson's orphanages in Mexico, Haiti, and Honduras in construction, in dormitories as dorm directors, in food preparation and general office support. Volunteers are also needed at an extension site in Yarnell, Arizona, where orphans from Mexico, Honduras and Haiti study intensive English for one year. Volunteers are needed there as teachers of English (no experience necessary), to supervise and work with students in food service and maintenance. Placements are for one year. Volunteers pay travel expenses; room and board are provided.

Frontier Internship in Mission
International Coordinating Office
150 Route de Ferney
P.O. Box 66
1211 Geneva 2, SWITZERLAND

FIM is an international ecumenical program that provides people age 35 or younger with the opportunity to work abroad on social and theological issues for a period of two years. This is followed by one year of re-integration work when the intern returns home. Interns throughout the world are sent from an organization in their own country to work with one based in another nation. A relationship between the two organizations is developed through the intern who works on one of three "frontier" issue areas: economic injustice, resurgence of religion, and the juxtaposition of cultures. Travel and modest living expenses are paid by the coordinating office.

Global Reach
6075 Romany Road
Oakland, CA 94618
(415) 653-6142

Global Reach interns are assigned to a remote Thai or Kenyan village where they teach math, English or science in a school and take on the responsibility of completing at least one community project. The internship is designed for college students 18-22 years old. Placement is for ten weeks between June and August. Interns may choose to live in a traditional family dwelling or with one of the school's full-time teachers. Tuition is $3,000 to be paid by the intern. Scholarships are available.

Global Volunteers
2000 American National Bank Building
St. Paul, MN 55101
(612) 228-9751

Global Volunteers forms teams of 8 to 12 volunteers who live in rural communities and work with villagers on development projects selected by the host community. The projects may involve construction and renovation of schools and clinics, health care, tutoring, business planning or assisting in other local activities. Opportunities are available in Guatemala, Mexico, Paraguay, Jamaica, India, and Western Samoa. Volunteers are of all ages and come from all backgrounds and occupations, including teachers, carpenters, homemakers, physicians, and artists. No special skills or languages are required. Trips range from $1,065 to $3,040 and include costs of training, visas, ground transportation, hotels, village lodging, food, and airfare from gateway cities.

Habitat for Humanity
Habitat and Church Streets
Americus, GA 31709
(912) 924-6935

HFH places volunteers for three-year periods in Africa, Asia, Latin America, and the Pacific Islands. The volunteers work on the organization, construction, and management of HFH housing projects. Volunteers must be 21 years or older. They receive a monthly stipend, housing, health insurance, and travel expenses. Volunteer construction opportunities are also available at 435 projects in the U.S., and in other capacities at the national headquarters in Americus. Volunteers for U.S. service must be 18 years or older. They receive training, free room and a $25 weekly stipend.

Institute for International Cooperation and Development
P.O. Box 103
Williamstown, MA 01267
(413) 458-9466

IICD organizes study and travel courses in Central America, Europe and the Soviet Union and solidarity work in Angola, Mozambique, Namibia, Nicaragua and Brazil. All programs are nine months long and include two months of residential training in language, cultural and economic studies, five months abroad, and two final months of public education work through presentations, writings and videos. Costs range from $5,000 to $8,000. Program is open to anyone 18 and older. Some financial aid is available as well as fundraising ideas.

Institute for Transportation and Development Policy
P.O. Box 56538
Washington, D.C. 20011
(301) 589-1810

Through their various projects (Bikes Not Bombs in Nicaragua, Mobility Haiti, and Bikes for Africa in Mozambique), the Institute provides bikes (for use in transporting both people and goods), bike parts, and technical assistance to local people in the community and to development, health-care, and literacy workers. ITDP also works with other local organizations and emerging bicycle industries in these three countries. Volunteers in local chapters in the United States (England and Canada) collect and ship donated bicycles for reconditioning in the workshops abroad. Overseas volunteers must have bike repair and maintainance experience and be able to speak Spanish, Portuguese, or French. Small business experience would be helpful. Length of service is flexible and volunteers should expect to pay their own expenses. Initial inquiries should be in writing.

Institute of Cultural Affairs
4220 N. 25th Street
Phoenix, AZ 85016
(602) 955-4811

or

206 E. Fourth Stret
New York, NY 10009
(212) 475-5020

or
4750 N. Sheridan Road
Chicago, IL 60640
(312) 769-6363

Volunteers are placed with community development organizations in Europe, Western U.S., Latin America, Southeast Asia and Africa. They may work directly with residents in development projects in programs dealing with health, agriculture, small industries, etc., or may act as support staff for the development team in residence, performing clerical, translation or funding tasks. Minimum duration of assignment is nine months. Most countries require familiarity with local language. Costs depend upon location, with room and board ranging from $76 to $250/month. Volunteers are responsible for their own expenses, including travel, room and board. Requests for information should be addressed to your nearest office.

Interfaith Office on Accompaniment
Box 77, Cardinal Station
Washington, D.C. 20064
(202) 635-5552

The Interfaith Office sends religious delegations to accompany displaced refugees to repatriation areas in El Salvador and to make follow-up visits to these reestablished communities. At least some members of the delegation must speak Spanish. The Interfaith Office encourages establishment of a long-term commitment between the delegates' and the Salvadoran community, such as a "sister" relationship, economic support, and the delegates' performance of community education work in this country on the situation in El Salvador. The size of the delegation and length of stay will depend on the mission. Delegates are expected to pay for their own expenses, plus a facilitation fee to the Interfaith office.

International Health Institute
Box G, BioMed Center, 4th Floor
Brown University
Providence, RI 02912
(401) 863-1186

Health professionals and students in health-related fields assist institutions in China, the Philippines, Mexico, Brazil, Nicaragua, Tanzania and Uganda in training indigenous people in primary health care and research techniques. Volunteers are placed to fill the requests of the host country. Ability to speak the local language would be helpful. Length of service is two weeks to a year. Volunteers usually pay expenses.

International Voluntary Services
1424-16th Street, N.W., Suite 204
Washington, D.C. 20036-2211
(202) 387-5533

IVS recruits technical assistance volunteers for small-scale rural development projects in Bangladesh, Bolivia, Ecuador, Zaire and Zimbabwe. Volunteers serve in the fields of agriculture, public health, small enterprise, cooperative development, and organizational management. Period of service is two to three years. Prerequisites include a college degree in the technical field and at least two years' work experience in a developing country in the field of expertise. Assignments in Latin America require fluency in Spanish. Assignments in Africa and Bangladesh require fluency in English and an interest in learning local languages. Room, board and travel expenses are provided.

Interplast
1731 Embarcadero, Suite 202
Palo Alto, CA 94303
(415) 424-0123

Interplast sends medical volunteers who can perform reconstructive surgery to Ecuador, Colombia, Peru, Honduras, Mexico, Africa, Western Samoa, the Philippines, Jamaica, Chile, and Nepal. Positions are for plastic surgeons, anesthesiologists, operating room nurses, pediatricians and recovery nurses. Placements are for two weeks. Spanish is desirable, but not required. Doctors in private practice are encouraged to pay their own transportation; otherwise transportation and housing are covered.

MADRE
121 West 27th Street, Room 301
New York, NY 10001
(212) 627-0444

MADRE places women professionals trained in midwifery, obstetrics, social work and stress counseling in Nicaragua. Volunteers provide service and conduct training. Placements range from one to two weeks. Spanish fluency is preferred. Volunteers pay all expenses.

Maestros por la Paz
2440-16th Street, #230
San Francisco, CA 94103
(415) 863-2431

Maestros sends volunteers to Nicaragua to teach English to professionals, scientists, technicians, and other adults. Volunteers must have teaching experience, though not necessarily teaching English, and be able to speak Spanish. Assignments are either from February to June or from August to December. A $40 monthly stipend is provided. Volunteers should expect to pay their own expenses.

Marin Interfaith Task Force
1024 Sir Francis Drake Boulevard
San Anselmo, CA 94960
(415) 454-0818

Volunteers are sent to San Salvador to accompany members of the non-governmental Human Rights Commission, providing an international presence to discourage human rights abuses against Commission members. Volunteers must be 21 years or older, fluent in Spanish, and fully knowledgeable about Salvadoran issues. Legal experience is useful. Volunteers pay all expenses associated with the two- to six-month stay.

Maryknoll Lay Missioners
Bethany Building
Maryknoll, NY 10545
(914) 762-6364

Lay missioners serve for three and a half years in Asia, Africa or Latin America. All new Lay Missioners attend a four-month Orientation to Mission Program at Maryknoll, New York, prior to leaving for their overseas assignment. If needed, language training is available in the country of assignment. Opportunities include community organization, health promotion, teaching, adult education, human rights and pastoral team ministry. Applicants must have a college degree or needed skill, plus a minimum of one year experience after completion of formal training. Applicants must also be Roman Catholic. Room, board, health and travel expenses are paid by Maryknoll, as well as a stipend.

Mennonite Central Committee
21 South 12th Street
Akron, PA 17501-0500
(717) 859-1151

MCC is the development and relief agency of Mennonite and Brethren in Christ churches. Currently more than 1,000 volunteers serve in agriculture, health, education, social services and community development in 50 countries, including the United States and Canada. Qualifications depend on assignment. Transportation, living expenses and a small stipend are provided. MCC asks that volunteers be Christian, actively involved in a church congregation, and agree to its nonviolent principles. Placements are for three years overseas, two years in North America.

Mennonite Voluntary Service
(See listing under U.S. Voluntary Service Organizations)

Mission Volunteers/USA
Mission Volunteers/Overseas
Presbyterian Church (USA)
100 Witherspoon Street
Louisville, KY 40202-1396
(502) 569-5300

MV helps church-supported organizations and projects find full-time volunteers both within the United States (including Alaska) and overseas. International assignments usually involve teaching and health care in Latin America, Africa, and Asia. Volunteers must be Christian and members of a church, though not necessarily Presbyterian. Room and board are provided with each assignment.

Nicaragua Network
2025 "I" Street, N.W., Suite 1117
Washington, D.C. 20006
(202) 223-2328

The Nicaragua Network organizes volunteer work brigades to help rebuild the country and experience Nicaraguan realities first-hand. Volunteers pick coffee, plant trees or do construction work while living and working alongside Nicaraguans. Spanish is helpful although not essential.

Operation Crossroads Africa
475 Riverside Drive
New York, NY 10011
(212) 242-8550

Crossroads operates rural African self-help projects in community health, agriculture, construction, anthropology, and archaelogy. The focus is on cross-cultural understanding through living and working with Africans. Any individual 18 years or older is eligible. Crossroads also operates a Caribbean program for 14-17 year olds who work in activities similar to those in the African projects. Knowlegde of French is required for some assignments. Limited financial assistance is available.

Overseas Development Network
2940-16th Street, Suite 110
San Francisco, CA 94103
(415) 431-4204

or

P.O. Box 1430
Cambridge, MA 02238
(617) 868-3002

ODN is a national network of university-based student groups working to promote long-term solutions to poverty through education and direct aid. ODN offers college students three- to nine-month internships in Latin America, Asia, Africa, the Middle East, and the United States. Proficiency in Spanish is required for the Latin American program. Interns work with community organizations, supporting local initiatives for economic development. They return to their schools to help educate others on third world problems and solutions. Expenses are paid by interns. Some financial assistance is available based on need.

Peace Brigades International
Central America Projects Office
193 Yonge Street, Suite 502
Toronto, Ontario, CANADA M5B 1M8
(416) 594-0429

PBI sends nonviolent/nonpartisan peace teams to El Salvador and Guatemala to monitor human rights violations. Volunteers accompany threatened individuals, partake in conflict resolution, and, upon their return, conduct public education programs. Volunteers must be fluent in Spanish, trained in nonviolence, and knowledgeable about Central American politics. Volunteers pay transportation and health insurance. Other expenses are covered by PBI.

Plenty USA
P.O. Box 2306
Davis, CA 95617

Plenty sponsors a limited number of volunteers for work on community-based development projects in food production, health, construction, and other village-scale appropriate technologies in Central America, the Caribbean and the U.S. The length of service varies with each position. No special requirements or language skills, but volunteers must pay travel and living expenses.

Science for the People
3217 College Avenue
Berkeley, CA 94705
(415) 652-6361

or

897 Main Street
Cambridge, MA 02139
(617) 547-0370

The Science for Nicaragua project of Science for the People sends educators and scientists to teach and supervise research in a Nicaraguan university or water resource agency. Applicants must have at least a bachelors degree in science or equivalent training and experience. The programs are one year in duration. Spanish fluency is required. A $100 per month stipend is provided; all other expenses are paid by the volunteer.

Service Civil International
c/o Innisfree Village
Route 2, Box 506
Crozet, VA 22932
(804) 823-1826

SCI organizes work camps in the United States, Europe, Asia and Africa to promote cross-cultural understanding and international peace. Volunteers work on environmental, construction, solidarity and social service projects and live together in simple quarters for two to three weeks. Volunteers must be 16 or older for U.S. workcamps, 18 or older for a European camp, and at least 21 and have SCI workcamp experience for a project in Africa or Asia. Volunteers pay travel expenses and SCI covers room, board and accident insurance. Many workcamps are accessible to disabled people and families.

Tecnica
3254 Adeline Street
Berkeley, CA 94703
(415) 655-3838

Skilled volunteers from the United States, Canada, England and other countries work in Nicaragua and with the African National Congress, South West Africa People's Organization, and in the frontline states of Southern Africa. Mechanics, engineers, computer and health professionals, teachers, agronomists, communications specialists, and others are needed for training and consulting assignments lasting from two weeks to three months or longer. Spanish-speaking ability is preferred for placements in Nicaragua, but is not required. Tecnica arranges room and board and the volunteer pays travel expenses. Some low-income scholarships are available.

Volunteers for Peace, Inc.
43 Tiffany Road
Belmont, VT 05730
(802) 259-2759

Volunteers for Peace coordinates work brigades throughout the world. Ten to twenty people from four or more countries join together to support community projects in the fields of construction, restoration, the environment, social services, agriculture, and archeology. VFP serves as an information and referral center for these international opportunities. Volunteers pay their own expenses, including an administration fee.

Volunteers in Asia
P.O. Box 4543
Stanford, CA 94309
(415) 723-3228

At the request of Asian institutions, Volunteers in Asia places undergraduates and recent graduates in English Teaching and English Resource positions in Asian countries. (We have no placements in Thailand or Nepal.) Volunteers must reside in the Santa Cruz or San Francisco Bay Area one year prior to overseas placement and must attend a five-month part-time preparation and training program at Stanford University. Volunteers pay an initial participant fee, and the hosting institution provides an in-country stipend for basic living expenses.

Volunteers in Overseas Cooperative Assistance
50 F Street, N.W., Suite 1075
Washington, D.C. 20001
(202) 626-8750

VOCA is a private, nonprofit organization which, under the aegis of its Cooperative Assistance and Farmer-to-Farmer programs, sends, on a volunteer basis, experienced professionals in cooperative development and agriculture to developing countries to provide short-term technical assistance to cooperatives (housing, rural electrification, credit unions and agriculture) and to private or governmental agricultural organizations. Projects usually run from one to three months. Volunteers are generally retired cooperative executives, university professors and highly experienced agriculturalists. VOCA pays all expenses and includes spouses on assignments over one month.

Volunteers Workcamp Association of Ghana/VOLU
P.O. Box 1540
Accra, GHANA

VOLU, one of Africa's oldest and largest workcamp agencies, recruits volunteers from Europe, the United States and countries around Africa (including Ghana itself) to work on projects such as building schools and roads, planting trees, etc., during the summer and winter holidays. No special skills are required. Volunteers are asked to pay $100 to cover food and board costs, plus their own travel expenses. Camps usually last about three weeks, and volunteers may participate in more than one.

Witness for Peace
P.O. Box 567
Durham, NC 27702
(919) 688-5049

Volunteers with WFP, a faith-based organization, live in communities throughout rural Nicaragua, making a one-year commitment that is renewable. Volunteers live and work with the Nicaraguan people, learning from them, sharing in their faith, and building relationships that foster peace and justice between the United States and Nicaragua. In coordination with WFP Stateside, volunteers work to change U.S. foreign policy by witnessing and documenting the effects of that policy, and by enabling an ever-broadening group of U.S. citizens to travel to Nicaragua to know for themselves. Volunteers document contra attacks and human rights violations, the results of U.S. "low intensity warfare" on the people, and the development of the peace process there. Volunteers lead short-term delegations and provide a permanent presence in areas of conflict. Volunteers must be U.S. citizens, 21 years of age or older, Spanish speaking, and committed to nonviolence. Volunteers pay costs of round-trip travel, language school (if necessary), and attempt to raise $1,000 for WFP to help cover living expenses. WFP covers medical expenses, provides room, board and travel within Nicaragua, and pays a $50 monthly stipend to volunteers.

World Teach
Phillips Brooks House, Harvard University
Cambridge, MA 02138
(617) 495-5527

American, Canadian and other college graduates are sent to Africa, Costa Rica, the People's Republic of China, Thailand, Poland, and other countries for a one-year teaching commitment in secondary schools. Volunteers in Africa teach classes (in English) in natural and social sciences, mathematics, art, and home economics, and participate in other school activities. In Costa Rica, China, and Thailand, volunteers teach English as a foreign language. The volunteer pays a fee which covers the cost of round-trip airfare, health insurance, orientation, field support, and program administration (estimated at $2,950-$3,450). The host school, community, or government provides housing and a monthly salary at least equivalent to that of local teachers (estimated at $72-$150). World Teach provides fundraising ideas for volunteers.

U.S. Voluntary Service Organizations

Working overseas is not the only way to gain community development experience. In many areas of the United States people face conditions of poverty similar to those found in the third world. Voluntary service in the United States can offer a low-cost opportunity for building solid credentials towards a career in community development.

ACORN
300 Flatbush Avenue
Brooklyn, NY 11217
(718) 789-5600

Acorn is a multi-racial membership organization of low-income families working to gain power within institutions that affect their everyday lives. Volunteers work as grassroots organizers throughout the United States. They receive a salary and must commit to one year of service. A working knowledge of Spanish and previous organizing experience are preferred, but not required.

Brethren Volunteer Services
(See listing under International Voluntary Service Organizations)

Center for Third World Organizing
3861 Martin Luther King, Jr., Way
Oakland, CA 94609
(415) 654-9601

CTWO is a research and training center working on issues affecting third world communities in the United States. A summer apprenticeship program for minority activists provides training and field experience for young people of color who are involved in social change work. The eight-week program trains 40 people, primarily college students, each summer in the techniques of community organizing. Volunteers for this program receive free room and a stipend. Other internships are sometimes available, including research and writing for the Center newsletter.

Citizen Action
2000 P Street, N.W., Suite 310
Washington, D.C. 20036
(202) 775-0370

Citizen Action is a national membership organization of people working for social change. Volunteers work as field organizers and fundraisers around issues such as foreign policy, energy, toxic waste, insurance reform, and health care. Excellent verbal communication and good interpersonal skills and commitment to progressive issues are required. Placements vary from six months to one year. Volunteers receive a stipend.

Farm Hands-City Hands
Green Chimneys
Putnam Lake Road
Brewster, NY 10509
(914) 279-2996 or (212) 892-6810

Green Chimneys has opportunities for volunteers to work at its farm school for emotionally disturbed children and children with learning disabilities. For work at the school and farm, room and board are provided. Green Chimneys' Farmhands-City Hands program can also provide a list of farms in New York, New Jersey and Connecticut that take volunteers. Volunteers assist in farm activities, learning firsthand the realities of family farming in the United States. Farm skills are usually taught by the host farmer. Placements last for approximately one and a half months or longer. Room, board, and a small stipend are usually provided, but arrangements are made between volunteer and farmer.

Father Wasson's Orphans
(See listing under International Voluntary Service Organizations)

Habitat for Humanity
(See listing under International Voluntary Service Organizations)

Institute for Transportation and Development Policy
(See listing under International Voluntary Service Organizations)

Institute of Cultural Affairs
(See listing under International Voluntary Service Organizations)

Jesuit Volunteer Corps
P.O. Box 23404
Oakland, CA 94623
(415) 465-5016

Volunteers are placed throughout the United States for periods of one year to work with poor and marginalized people. They serve as teachers, nurses, counselors, social workers, and as assistants on projects defined by local need. Volunteers live modestly in a cooperative household with other JVC volunteers. Hosting organization provides room and board, travel expenses, and a $75 monthly stipend. Volunteers are usually at least 21 years old, have a college degree, and are motivated by Christian principles.

Los Niños
1330 Continental Street
San Ysidro, CA 92073
(619) 661-6912

Los Niños is a nonprofit organization providing long-term community development programs in the four areas of school teaching, nutrition, family gardens and literacy. The above programs are carried out by volunteers serving one-year placements. The programs facilitate self-reliance and provide education for social awareness. The cost of the program varies with the length of stay and whether or not the volunteer chooses to live at the Los Niños facility. Also offered are weekend and week-long programs to U.S. participants who want to learn more about development along the U.S.-Mexico border.

Lutheran Volunteer Corps
1226 Vermont Avenue, N.W.
Washington D.C. 20005
(202) 387-3222

This is a domestic program which places volunteers in the eastern states for a period of one year. (Other offices are located in Baltimore and Wilmington, Delaware; Washington, D.C.; Chicago and Milwaukee.) Volunteers work through agencies dealing in the areas of direct service, public policy, advocacy, community organizing, and education. Volunteers share housing with three to seven others. Travel, room and board, medical coverage, and daily work-related transportation expenses are supplied. The program is open to people from all traditions of Christian faith.

Marianist Voluntary Service Community
P.O. Box 9224
Wright Brothers Branch
Dayton, OH 45409
(513) 229-3287

Volunteers are placed for one year commitments in urban areas in Kentucky, New York and Ohio. Placements include social work and community organizing, health care and housing rehabilitation. Volunteers must be at least 20 years of age, possess skills appropriate to placement, and be able to pay transportation expenses to and from the city. The organization provides a stipend.

Mennonite Central Committee
(See listing under International Voluntary Service Organizations)

Mennonite Voluntary Service
722 Main Street
P.O. Box 347
Newton, KS 67114-0347
(316) 283-5100

MVS helps meet the needs of poor and disadvantaged people in the United States and Canada. Volunteer placements range from staffing food banks and emergency assistance centers to working with migrant farmworkers. Social work, community organization, housing rehabilitation, and education skills are in particular demand. Initial terms of two years are strongly encouraged, though some assignments are available for one year. Spanish is helpful or required for some positions. Volunteers must be of a Christian denomination and at least 18 years old. All expenses are covered by MVS.

Mission Volunteers/USA
(See listing under International Voluntary Service Organizations)

Plenty USA
(See listing under International Voluntary Service Organizations)

Proyecto Libertad
306 East Jackson, 3rd Floor
Harlingen, TX 78551
(512) 425-9552

Proyecto Libertad is a legal office on the Texas-Mexico border representing Central American refugees. Working with Central Americans in detention, including minors, PL provides legal services and advocacy, helping them apply for political asylum, raise bond money, contact relatives, and understand the U.S. legal system. PL also participates in federal litigation to protect refugee rights. Volunteers work in Harlingen and at the detention center on all aspects of the program. Volunteers must speak Spanish and have a knowledge of Central American politics. A car would also be extremely useful. Volunteers cover their own expenses, but some assistance may be available.

Quaker Volunteer Witness Program
101 Quaker Hill Drive
Richmond, IN 47374
(317) 962-7573

Volunteers serve for one year beginning in September in U.S. communities. Placements begin with a one-week orientation program in Richmond, Indiana. Programs include inner-city ministry, peace and disarmament, refugee assistance, services to the poor and elderly, evangelical outreach, and administrative support. Most positions are intended for generalists, but some require Spanish or teaching credentials. All expenses except transportation to the orientation program are covered.

Service Civil International
(See listing under International Voluntary Service Organizations)

Sioux Indian YMCAs
P.O. Box 218
Dupree, SD 57623
(605) 365-5232

Volunteers of college age or older are needed to serve for two months during the summer as camp staff at Leslie Marrowbone Memorial YMCA Camp, working with 8- to 14-year-old Sioux children. Also needed are community work volunteers to live in small isolated Sioux communities to support various youth and family projects. These placements are from four to ten weeks, year round. Volunteers must have camp or community work skills, be flexible and able to share their own culture, as well as relate to another. The YMCA can help with the expenses of room and board.

United Farm Workers
P.O. Box 62, La Paz
Keene, CA 93570
(805) 822-5571

The UFW works for justice for farm workers and for safe food for consumers. Volunteers spend one year or more in rural or urban areas, organizing farm workers and consumers. Opportunities are also available in computer-related and administrative capacities. Volunteers receive room and board and a small stipend.

Ursuline Companions in Mission
323 East 198th Street
Bronx, NY 10458
(212) 365-7410

Christian volunteers are sent to inner-city and rural work sites in the United States to provide education, social work, outreach to the elderly, health care, and pastoral ministry. Volunteers must be 21 years or older and possess skills compatible with needs of specific ministries.

Witness for Peace
(See listing under International Voluntary Service Organizations)

Study Tours & Alternative Travel

There are a number of groups that conduct "reality tours" in the third world. These are socially responsible educational tours that provide participants firsthand experience of the political, economic and social structures that create or sustain hunger, poverty and environmental degradation. These tours offer an opportunity to meet with people from diverse sectors and with various perspectives on issues of agriculture, development and the environment. They often include the opportunity to stay with local people, visit rural areas and meet with grassroots organizers, and can deepen your understanding of hunger and poverty in the third world. The experience and insights gained on such a tour may influence your future work for democratic social change.

African American Heritage Study Association
19 South La Salle Street, Suite 301
Chicago, IL 60603
(312) 443-0929

Each year the Association offers a variety of study tours throughout Africa. Past tour themes have included the economic and political development of frontline states and the role of women in the family. Tours are led by experts in African studies.

Center for Global Education
Augsburg College
731 - 21st Avenue South
Minneapolis, MN 55454
(612) 330-1159

The Center for Global Education plans and coordinates travel seminars to Central America, the Caribbean, the Philippines and the Middle East. The goal of the seminars is to introduce participants to the reality of poverty and injustice in the third world. Tours for church groups focus on the role of the church and the responsibility of Christians in working for social change. Other tours focus on food and agriculture, women, and human rights issues.

Global Exchange
2141 Mission Street, #202
San Francisco, CA 94110
(415) 255-7296

Global Exchange hosts Reality Tours that offer a unique opportunity to learn firsthand about pressing issues confronting the third world. Tour participants meet with peasants, labor organizers, religious leaders, peace activists, environmentalists, scholars, and government officials. Countries where tours have been conducted in the past or are planned include Brazil, Haiti and the Dominican Republic, Guatemala, El Salvador, Honduras, Nicaragua, Israel and Palestine, India and the Philippines, Zimbabwe and Mozambique, as well as Appalachia and the U.S.-Mexico border.

Los Niños
(See listing under U.S. Voluntary Service Organizations)

Marazul Tours, Inc.
50 West 57th Street, Suite 1311
New York, NY 10107
(212) 582-9570

Marazul Tours is a well-known coordinator of alternative tours to Central America. Many of the organizations in this guide enlist Marazul's expertise in planning trips to Cuba, El Salvador, Guatemala, and Nicaragua. Marazul's own study tours are planned for Argentina, Brazil, Colombia, El Salvador, Guatemala, Mexico, and Uruguay.

Our Developing World
13004 Paseo Presada
Saratoga, CA 95070
(408) 379-4431

ODW has led study tours to Cuba, Nicaragua, Honduras, Mozambique, Zimbabwe, the Philippines, and Hawaii. The tours provide an opportunity to talk with peasants, workers, women's associations, health workers, and co-op members, as well as a chance to learn about health, human rights and educational campaigns, agrarian reform, and economic and social planning. ODW conducts study tours only and does not offer volunteer overseas work opportunities.

Plowshares Institute
P.O. Box 243
Simsbury, CT 06070
(203) 651-4304

Plowshares tours aim at initiating cross-cultural dialogue between first and third world peoples. Participants must commit to advance preparation and community education work upon their return. Trip itineraries include meetings with religious and civic leaders, home-stay experiences, and visits to development projects. The Institute plans two- to three-week programs to Africa, South and Southeast Asia, India, Australia and the South Pacific.

Servas
11 John Street, Suite 706
New York, NY 10038
(212) 267-0252

Servas is an international cooperative system of hosts and travelers established to help build world peace by providing opportunities for personal contact among people of diverse cultures and backgrounds. Hosts offer international travelers housing, meals, or company (terms are set by each individual), and U.S. travelers receive the same when traveling abroad. The program is designed to strengthen the people-to-people links in the peace movement.

Venceremos Brigade
National Office
P.O Box 673
New York, NY 10035

or

P.O. Box 7739
Oakland, CA 94601

Venceremos Brigade participants travel for two weeks in Cuba, visiting schools, factories, clinics, and hospitals; attending musical and cultural programs; having informal visits and discussions with Cubans; and participating in educational seminars with representatives from other countries. Two or three of those days may include actual work brigade activities. Participants must be at least 18 years old, U.S. citizens, and not currently in the military service. They are expected to pay all transportation, room and board, and miscellaneous expenses, but scholarships are available.

References

Organizations

Council on International Educational Exchange and Commission on Voluntary Service and Action, P.O. Box 768, Yarmouth, ME 04096.

Institute of International Education, 809 United Nations Plaza, New York, NY 10017.

St. Vincent Pallotti Center, 715 Monroe Street, N.E., Washington, D.C. 20017-1755.

Guides to International Voluntary Service

Connections: A Directory of Lay Volunteer Service Opportunities, St. Vincent Pallotti Center, 715 Monroe Street, N.E., Washington, D.C. 20017-1755. (202) 529-3330. Free publication.

International Directory for Youth Internships, Learning Resources in International Studies, 777 United Nations Plaza, New York, NY 10017.

International Workcamp Directory, VFP International Workcamps, 43 Tiffany Road, Belmont, VT 05730.

Overseas Development Network Opportunities Catalog, Opportunities in International Development in New England, Career Opportunities in International Development, Overseas Development Network, P.O. Box 1430, Cambridge, MA 02238, (617) 868-3002.

Overseas List: Opportunities for Living and Working in Developing Countries, Augsburg Publishing House, 426 Fifth Street, Box 1209, Minneapolis, MN 55440.

Transitions Abroad, 18 Hulst Road, Box 344, Amherst, MA 01004.

Travel Programs in Central America, Central America Information Center, P.O. Box 50211-W, San Diego, CA 92105.

U.S. Nonprofit Organizations in Development Assistance Abroad, ACVAFS, 200 Park Avenue South, New York, NY 10003.

VITA News, Volunteers in Technical Assistance, 1815 North Lynn Street, Suite 200, Arlington, VA 22209-2079.

Volunteer! The Comprehensive Guide to Voluntary Service in the U.S. and Abroad, Commission on Voluntary Service and Action, P.O. Box 347, Newton, KS 67114.

Who's Involved With Hunger: An Organization Guide for Education and Advocacy, by Patricia L. Kutzner and Nicola Lagoudakis, with Teresa Eyring. World Hunger Education Service, 3018 - 4th Street, N.E., Washington, D.C. 20017.

Work, Study, Travel Abroad: The Whole World Handbook, prepared by the Council on International Educational Exchange and published by St. Martin's Press Council on International Educational Exchange, 205 E. 42nd Street, New York, NY 10017, (212) 661-1414 Ext 61108.

Guides to U.S. Voluntary Service

Community Jobs, 1516 P Street, N.W., Washington, D.C. 20005.

Invest Yourself, Commission on Voluntary Service and Action, 475 Riverside Drive, Room 665, New York, NY 10027.

Good Works: A Guide to Careers in Social Change, by Joan Anzalore, ed. Dembner Books (distributed by W.W. Norton & Co., Inc., 500 Fifth Avenue, New York, NY 10110).

Educational Materials

Aid as Obstacle: Twenty Questions About Our Foreign Aid and the Hungry, by Frances Moore Lappé, Joseph Collins, and David Kinley. Institute for Food and Development Policy, 1981.

Aid: Rhetoric and Reality, by Teresa Hayter and Catherine Watson. Pluto Press, 1985.

Betraying the National Interest, by Frances Moore Lappé, Rachel Schurman, and Kevin Danaher. Institute for Food and Development Policy, 1988.

Beyond Charity: U.S. Voluntary Aid for a Changing Third World, by John G. Sommer. Overseas Development Council, 1977.

Don't Be Afraid, Gringo: A Honduran Woman Speaks From the Heart, edited and translated by Medea Benjamin. Harper & Row, 1989.

Help or Hindrance? United States Economic Aid in Central America, by Kevin Danaher. Institute for Food and Development Policy, 1987.

In the Name of Progress: The Underside of Foreign Aid, by Patricia Adams and Lawrence Solomon. Energy Probe, 1986.

The Philippines: Fire on the Rim, by Joseph Collins. Institute for Food and Development Policy, 1989.

Volunteering in the Third World: What's at Stake? a 1986 videotaped discussion on the politics of the Peace Corps. Overseas Development Network, P.O. Box 2306, Stanford, CA 94305.

Publications on Traveling and Tourism

Alternative Tourism: A Resource Book, Ecumenical Coalition on Third World Tourism (ECTWT), P.O. Box 9-25, Bankhen, Bangkok 110900, Thailand.

Contours (Concern for Tourism Magazine), Ecumenical Coalition on Third World Tourism, P.O. Box 9-25, Bankhen, Bangkok 110900, Thailand.

Directory of Alternative Travel Resources 1988, by Dianne G. Brause, One World Family Travel Network, P.O. Box 3417, Berkeley, CA 94703 (415) 841-TRIP, $7.00 postpaid.

One World Family Travel Network, 81868 Lost Valley Lane, Dexter, OR 97431.

Visions of Poverty, Visions of Wealth: Tourism in the Third World, New Internationalist (December 1984), 113 Atlantic Avenue, Boston, MA 11201.

Index to Organizations